Past Forward to
FAITH
and
LOVE

PAST FORWARD TO
FAITH
and
LOVE

ROD HUNT

authorHOUSE®

AuthorHouse™
1663 Liberty Drive
Bloomington, IN 47403
www.authorhouse.com
Phone: 1 (800) 839-8640

Published by AuthorHouse   10/09/2015

ISBN: 978-1-5049-5491-4 (sc)
ISBN: 978-1-5049-5490-7 (e)

Print information available on the last page.

Any people depicted in stock imagery provided by Thinkstock are models, and such images are being used for illustrative purposes only.
Certain stock imagery © Thinkstock.

This book is printed on acid-free paper.

DEDICATION

This book is dedicated to the memories of some of my loved ones departed; to those, even in their absence, who still resonate in my mind and are still pushing me to be the best man that I can be: Big Mama (Great grandmother), Mu (Grandmother), Mr. Floyd (Step Grandfather), Uncle Joe Pete, Uncle Hozea, Uncle Shorty Red, Aunt Totsie, Aunt Betty, and my Hood City brother, Eric Reed. We'll all meet in heaven soon. Much love.

ACKNOWLEDGMENTS

I thank God for giving me life and the gift of writing. I thank my parents, Albert and Felecia Hunt, for sticking together for all these years to make sure my sister and I knew that love is infinitely bigger and more important than anything we can imagine. I thank Candace Hunt for being that overprotective yet caring and close sister. I'm thankful for all my family and friends who have encouraged me through the years to keep writing. The list is too long to mention, but just know that I love you all. God bless.

PART 1

GAINING ON MY PAST

We all want progress. But progress means getting nearer to the place where you want to be. And if you have taken a wrong turning, then to go forward does not get you any nearer. If you are on the wrong road, progress means doing an about-turn and walking back to the right road; and in that case the man who turns back the soonest is the most progressive man.

—C. S. Lewis

MY SWEET, DEAR LIFE

I came in during the late nights with a staggered swag,
Giving you promises I couldn't keep.
Next morning, it was better to sleep in than to speak;
I got along better with you when I napped.
I ignored you when I did awake,
Then left you alone to fulfill my loneliness for lust's sake,
And I only worked to support our separation.
If unfulfilled, I called you a bitch to your face,
But I would smile if all my fronts were in place.
I didn't want you, yet you were to blame for my problems.
I saw you as useless and meaningless,
Then looked to those same words to try to solve them.
I didn't get you, so I spoke against you.
I didn't want to own up to you;
I just wanted to rent you
For special occasions, like the tuxedo for my wedding.
Our bonds were just rare formalities for show;
No wonder there were no tears of joy shedding,
Only tears of regrets after binges and selfish sex.
But I kept pledging allegiance to the bliss of ignorance,
And by noon the next day, it was you again; I would forget—
But you were always forgiving and never forgot me.
My unknown craving for loneliness caused me to get upset.

I didn't want you hounding me like an affable shadow,
Always standing ready to be accepted like a toast.
I was fine with my false hopes and dreams, my strife;
I was my own worst enemy, but I feared you the most.
You wanted to tear me away from my existence.
You wanted to claim me as if you were my wife,
But I kept running down the wrong road.
I ran and ran until I could run no more …
From my sweet, sweet dear life.

BLISSFUL REGRETS

Better now than I can ever remember,
Even as a prisoner of outdated lust,
I could update and regain my artificial freedom.
But I'm done talking and walking backward toward fuss and distrust.

I'm facing my crossroads like the man I was brought up to be,
Soul searching for the path purposed for me.
Had a habit of returning to that which always led to discomfort.
I was a dog with good intentions, but my digging was constant,
Always searching for the dirt that was softer.

It was part of my dreams to never live a fenced-in life,
Yet I was content with every link that surrounds me today.
So I pray; as I look around my acre of land and possessions,
I thank God for such a worthy spot to be stuck with regrets and
confessions.

Yet thoughts often tormented me of what I could've done,
If I would've done what I should've done.
I can't stop the wind from blowing in my face,
So I try to place hindsight into it while forward my mind runs.

I hope that I'm at least on par with my regrets at my next checkpoint
of life
(Or death, whichever's first).
Whether I'm helping load or riding in the back of a hearse,
I dream of moving toward more bliss while the regrets are buried.

The future hasn't been as scary, since my mind has been a little more settled,

And as long as I can still see it, in my own past, I'll probably still meddle.

But just like kindergarten was a blur by the twelfth,

My current footsteps will deteriorate with my restlessness.

The best has yet to come (or, shall I say, "I've yet to reach").

Until then, I'll try to settle for better, even when I think it's not better for me.

MOOD SWING SHIFT (DICKIE BLUES)

Had visions of professionalism toward the end of high school;
Probably could've been, but I wasn't exactly a scholar.
I still saw myself in spit-shined gators, sporting a creased white collar
    As I earned top dollar at the top of a skyscraper,
    Overlooking Decatur somewhere.
I was unaware that I was bound for steel-toed boots and Dickie blues.
How I got here is nothing new (and another story in itself),
    But these boots are mandatory on my current road to wealth.
My grind starts with me grabbing my flashlight and glove clip off
the shelf,
    Heading out my door into the late night.
My pickup and I set our sights toward the graveyard shift of the paper
industry.
Not a night goes by that wonder doesn't ask whether this was meant
for me;
I reach my destination only to feel caged like a freak in a basement
with no sympathy
    For those enjoying death's cousin or the nightlife,
    Being the freaks they want to be.
I sip caffeine and inhale a pollutant that's far from recreational.
    As I assist in operating global warmers,
    This is far from sensational,
    "But somebody's got to do it."
That's the cliché that helps me get through these nights
    And helps me sleep during the day.
That's my answer when people ask how I do it or when they say,
    "You're better than me. I wouldn't do it."

Yes, I make more than most teachers, but I've got less peace
     Than those who dreamed of their education degrees—
     And I don't get seasonal breaks.
During the summer, my skull is an oven on bake;
My brain is not on drugs anymore,
     So I'm trying to enjoy the rest of the cake
     That's left on my plate.
     On my days off,
I get time to enjoy a bit of normalcy
     (Which for me
     Is turning up those red-neck cans
     Quicker than a redneck can.)
Getting wiser with my buddy
But feeling like that lonely stoner in that song by Kid Cudi.

My mood swings toward the evening shift on a Friday;
     While most of the town is hitting the highway
     Toward their weekend plans,
     I'm giving up my sunshine
     In exchange for a pipe wrench placed in my hand.
To that man responsible for this shift: I don't like you.
This is like the menstrual cycle
     Of my months.
     The biggest rattler of my mind
     Makes me want to strike you.
It's funny how our moods can overrule that in which we truly
understand;

I overstand that I chose dirt over pavement.
Nowadays I'm trying to throw gravel over sand
    As I pace myself toward another day off.
Day shift is next, but my body is still addicted to the night.
My head fights with my pillow
    As my rest resists my bed's quest for a peaceful plight
    Toward new, deferred dreams.
Three hours of sleep are just not enough, it seems.
    I awake as if an earthquake just ended, and
Whatever damage has been done is going to have to wait
    Ten minutes to be tended to
    (And that's if I remember to push the snooze button).
Sometimes, I suddenly awake and realize that I didn't.
My day starts off with the temptation to lie
    And call my boss and tell him I'm bedridden,
But the strength that I pray for makes sure that my pickup and I hook
up once more.
Finally, a Friday that's easy to feel thankful for;
    As I back out with a grin
    That's longer than the week has been,
I get to set long weekend plans.
    And almost nothing can stop my happiness,
    Not even the fact that next Wednesday night,
    My Dickie blues start all over again.

JUST A MAN

Been a clone of myself,
My spirit put on hold.
My soul relies on my wealth (or a lack thereof).
Trying to look above for infinite peace and love,
But I can't seem to ignore what's in front of me.
The Hunt in me keeps me searching for what lies ahead,
But nothing always comes back to tell me that something said
Not to worry about it (or her)
And to keep my eyes high without the redness and Visine.
But here I go again, trying to look clean for this mean-bodied
Woman approaching. At a loss for words, but I'm hoping
She notices that my swag is as smooth as silk—
But I get overlooked like some milk
With too early an expiration date. But wait!
I was feeling like *the* man just a few seconds ago,
But I guess I'm just *a* man.

At times, I can be the funniest kid my little girls know;
These Generation Z kids don't have to ask too many whys.
Due to the X rated amounts they are already exposed to,
I'm forced to keep the man within, within reach.
And they tend to think that Daddy's rich,
But Daddy's just living beyond his blessings,
Trying to keep my Cadillac out of the ditch of repossession.
Self-hailed king trying not to be overthrown by overspending;
Had self-hailed queens sending me more questions than actions;
I'm just a man looking for a woman who doesn't dodge satisfaction.

I like to stand like an equator, but I'm only a tiny fraction of this world.

God and my phone list are what keep me from being homeless.

My bed sleeps like an ant's bed in His eyes.

I'm old news under the sun;

Unlike it, I'm not guaranteed to rise.

My appearances will eventually become dust under the dawn.

I'm aware of this

Yet it's still no fun without the flash beyond life's camera lens

Until nothingness sends that message again,

Telling us that we're just men.

Not always just, … but we're only men;

A … men.

BLOOD AND WATER

Blood and water are vital yet unreliable at times;
Blood can be too thick through the thin and too thin through the thick.
Rain is so now and then with its visits that water can seem so scarce.
Hell and impurities can accompany it when it does show up.
I try to filter it all, but flaws continue to spring up from the water into the blood;
The present ones are piled on top of the past.
I've started to feel really small, like a passenger on a toy train set,
Engaging in a game of circular emotions with the ones I chose to ride with.
My self is waiting, so I've decided to get off at the next stop.
We're going to find that train that only moves forward toward growth.
My blood will remain close at heart,
And family never had to answer when I called before I reached out again.
Though from now on, they'll have to catch me like the river flow is required.
I'm praying for soul control of my destiny;
God should be enough when the river is dry and my blood is too thin for me.

FAMILY CRIES

Where are the old days?

They've become memories too distant.

New ones aren't being made.

Tight schedules have killed closeness.

Appointments have to be set to talk via text.

On old photos, our smiles connect

Like brothers and sisters in a cheese factory.

Now it takes death to get a group photo,

Fabricated smiles like the member in the casket,

A photo that a click of the family won't be a part of.

Sides had to be taken …

Due to a member feeling slighted and unloved,

More verbal shoves than physical hugs.

Holidays are two- or three-hour buffets.

Our kids aren't even close enough to play like we did.

Now we won't, so they don't.

The elders still hold us together as much as they can.

Problem is that the backbones are gone.

It takes a miraculous act of God for us to be able to stand.

Where are the days of old?

When family was at the top of the list,

Backyard cookouts over the pit,

Low-country boils without the toil?

When it wasn't about eating the meal, then the highway.

When we had nothing, we had family.

The American dream got *us* doing things *my* way.

It was always some "Shut up and listen to what I say,"

But at least we were close enough to listen.

Now most of the time, if it's not a cash benefit,

We're not even paying attention.

Water has surpassed blood in thickness.

If it wasn't for social media,

We'd see sickness more than kin

Until death brings us together again,

And more memories are lowered into the sand.

The family reunion is at the repast:

Black suits, black dresses, macaroni, and fried chicken.

You're welcome to bring a friend.

QUESTIONS OF A CONFUSED LOVE

Not meaning to rush things,
But would it be fair to say that love lurks
In the atmosphere between us?
If so, or if not even,
What would you like to see before we could
Shape those four letters out of whatever it is
We're breathing …
So that they're verbalized when we exhale?
Is it something you're waiting to see in
Me … perhaps in yourself as well?
Other options feel more closed on my end,
Although they're officially open.
Do you feel the same way or more of the
Latter and maybe hoping
To see if something better strolls along by chance?
I'd like to see how reliable our first
Impressions are.
Are you concerned about what may lie
Behind those walls? Your view of mine
Or my view of yours?
Are you waiting for any old feelings to
Die down before allowing new love
To resurrect?
I've only got feelings for myself that I
Would like to share inside you.
Does this lovely progress we're making
Seem too good to be true?

Proudly I've never been able to separate sex from commitment.

My biggest problem has been committing

To sex before the shipment

Of love … Whipped is what it's called.

Lastly, are you willing to whip me

Before love gets all its answers,

Knowing that if you strip and slide down

My pole, that in my mind you're *my*

Personal dancer?

My options and club officially closed.

Is this what you want?

Could I be your only slave until and after

Love arrives?

Or does it depend on my performance?

I would expect to be the only slave to your mastery.

Do you think love would arrive

Under those conditions

Or, better yet, survive?

Let me know. Love is waiting.

AN ODELESS FAREWELL

I'm sorry, but we can be no more.
I know I've said this a trillion times before
And after,
So much so that it doesn't provide you laughter
Anymore. You just ignore
And give me that devilish yet sexy grin,
Like I'm your prisoner just rattling my chains again.
And maybe I am, but I'm not.
For you my flesh has been hot,
While my soul has become colder
And more saturated with a hatred that smolders.

There's no denying your power to turn my shy streak bolder,
You and Savannah Green.
Satan put you both in my way at the land where railroads cross.
Our threesome became official after my faith was lost
Within the romantic streets of Chatham County.
I inhaled her soundly
While I covered you with ruby red
In preparation to mix you with other desires in my head;
However, blissful memories and regrets are about dead.

Wisdom has since cut my ties with Savannah Green,

And I feel my blade getting wiser.

I try to limit my time with you,

But you call obsessively to dine with you.

We would agree to just one kiss,

Only to see plenty

Sips lead to a drowsy abyss,

Where worthwhile dreams are withered away.

Despite this,

God's grace and mercy motions me to see another day,

Still with the free will to live by faith or delusion.

You often sit so tempting in the middle near confusion,

Staring me down while patting your lust seat of profusion.

You're awesome in validating my illusions

Of heaven.

You're a visitor who's allowed to walk to your prisoner's cell,

Given access to warm my chest and make my head swell,

Yet your comfort is as temporary as the moonshine dwells.

You're just as hard to dodge as well,

But now it's morning time,

So go back to hell forever and farewell.

I think I'm ready to shine, … I think.

TOO MUCH BUT NOT ENOUGH

Too much thinking,
Too much blinking
In anxiety.
Too much drinking,
Wisdom swimming
Across the mind.
Not enough sinking
Into the pool of action.
Too much satisfaction
With crawling and lacking.
Too little patience
In God.
Too much patience
In self.
Potential on the shelf
Collecting dust
Instead of wealth.
Too many feelings felt,
Useless ones,
Too many emotions kept
Insecure and outdone,
Outrunning the race.
Be still more.

Not enough work.

Too much of the wrong types of fun.

Not enough peace with the storms.

Too much longing for the sun.

Long only for the Son of man.

In God, enough is enough.

Victory is already won.

FROM SOMETHING TO NOTHING

Wasn't born with a silver spoon, but it was silver plated.
Many of my wants never arrived,
But all my top-shelf needs seemed to have always made it
On time.
Yet my growth was stunted and my mind partially blind
To how much richer we were in spiritual guidance.

I had the assurance that my family's blessings were God approved,
That at least most were not misused
Or taken for granted.
Yet I confused grace, mercy, and favor with ambition implanted
Within my soul like granite.
I was hard up for the trivial fight,
Apparently not doing all wrong.
If asked, I could sincerely say I was doing all right.

But my sincere efforts were seared with sin,
Pride that blocked the dark tunnel to my true self.
I cared less about the mystical light of freedom at the end.
I wanted the illusions of wealth
Caked up on the walls,
A felon of time and money.
I ended up killing it all
For damaged internals and fancy externals.
Neighborhood friends called me "spoiled."
Yes, but my folks kept me within the fence of faith.
My disease of fashion designs was self-imposed and terminal.

While I used my spoils to rotten,
I'm sure there was another person somewhere
Who hadn't even gotten
Close to the change my family spared,
Yet who was content with nothing,
Trusting in the Lord like the birds are accustomed to
Living above sea level.
Peace was felt through the stomach rumblings,
Through the street wars outside their slum doors,
Patience in the soup kitchen lines,
Thankful for the cool draft in the holes of their pants,
Not custom cut for stylish design.
Someone who knew the value of giving back
Didn't hesitate to give God time
And a dime out of every irregular dollar he or she made,
Not for more dollars but for the spiritual sense laid
Within his or her soul.

While it took me
Ungratefulness,
Pride,
Greed,
Debt,
A broken twenty-five-hundred-square-foot home
To realize that the man who has the least
But owns the most faith is the greatest,
I used to think I was onto something.
I'm thankful I was brought down to my version of nothing.
Now I can get somewhere.

PART 2

ENTERING THE REALM OF LIFE

Righteousness deals with the past of my life that is now covered. Self-control deals with the present of my life as I face each day. Judgement deals with the future setting when I shall stand before God.

—Ravi Zacharias

CLOSET FAITH?

Knowing and doing are two different things.
What shall I do with the truth that's before me?
I ducked, dodged, sought, and found. Now what?
Do I become simply a tourist who witnessed Nazareth?
Take a few pictures to bolster the image of my home?
Collect some garments to make my disguise more eccentric?
Learn some dialect to appear wise during happy hour?
Become my small circle's validation of self-righteousness?
Will I keep this truth within sight at all times like my cell phone?
Or will I tuck it away when I receive a text from a tempter?

Not only can I now distinguish confusion, but it's also transparent.
Will I embrace the truth on the other side?
Or will I cover chaos with clothing of democracy?
People may look as though they're aware that I'm aware of something,
But they can receive only what I give them.
Will my words be a bundle of lies mixed with a false sense of hope,
Like the Hennessy and Coke in my glass?
Will my grins approve the quest of having sex without true
commitment?
Or will I allow truth to smother flaws and birth rebirth,
Eventually reaching the highest stages of earthly transition
And taking a few folks with me?

Or will I keep it between me and other believers,
Afraid of being ridiculed for trying to be what I was meant to be
Instead of who I'm not,
Switching back and forth from a cynic of deception to one of truth,
Believing that our souls don't affect each other's?
If this is believed, it's a piece of confusion that still blends in,
Or for some it's a known trick that we still treat ourselves with.

PLEASURE TRAPS

I love pleasure.
It's the traps of it I hate.
I'd rather fight freely within destiny
Than think I'm free
In the booby traps of fate,
Places where I just feel safe,
Feelings I chased while running in place.
Drank my lows to balance my highs.
Frustration … was flushing my weed a waste?
Entered some flesh to get a test taste of love
Above, within, feelings that aren't condoned.
I built a home from the ground up once.
Now I can't even claim it as my own,
Because the foundation was shaky.
My pleasure trap went from a shack
To a house I thought would make me happy.
Pleasure can be temporary like a perm.
Things can come back pretty nappy.
If I'm going to be in the valley of the shadows,
I need to learn how to sport a supernatural walk.

SOUL MATE MARKET

My soul isn't for rent, sale, or lease to buy,
But you're welcome to take a peep in
Whenever you like; or if you have a freedom
That's compatible, maybe we can set up an
Unconditional merger,
Something that will enhance each other
Instead of tearing one or both of us down.

I've cried, suffered, and worked too hard to
Just hand mine over, and the maintenance
Is ongoing; there's nothing more valuable
Than my soul. There's only an equivalent
Soul to match; I'm not interested in this
World's soul mate market.

I don't want anybody claiming mine to
Supplement the discomfort of hers,
Just to foreclose on because she can't
Keep up, … leaving me in a chaotic bid to
Get it back. She may want to borrow
My soul on those occasional
Nights when one of hers isn't
Sitting right, dirtying up my comforter
For me to have to suffer and reclean.

Please don't come with the front of
Wanting to set up a merger with your
Disguised first impressions. I'm on
God's watch, so I'll have time to read
Between the lines of your paperwork; plus
I'm aware that snakes are suburban
Creatures as well these days. Please
Don't waste the time that you're running
Out of.

I hope none of this sounds egotistical.
It's just that I try to keep my estate real
And beyond the worth of this world.
I realize some will try to depreciate me
So they can appreciate me within
Their realm of whateverness. I try to
Keep my soul as priceless as cleverness.

Satan has a monopoly on this world's
Soul mate market, but I'm not trying
To sell or buy into any of it. I'll hold
And continue building on what my
Family left me, cash it in upon death,
And make sure there's enough left
For my kids' kids or a possible spouse.
There's nothing free about this world's
Soul mate market, and I'm not looking
For a hidebound whorehouse.

TIED DEMONS

I have to make sure that I don't become
An individualist again.
I have to make sure that I'm truly being
A friend to those I call friends.
I have to be careful how I use my freedom.
New starts can aggravate old ends.
I have to be careful.
My demons are on leashes but ones that
May be invisible to some.
It may appear that I'm following stupidity,
Indistinguishable from the dumb.

UPSETTING THE BAR

While I sit at the bar,
A guy drunkenly asks, "Bro, you okay?"
I reply assuredly, "Good when I got here, and I'll leave how I came."
I wonder whether he could say the same.
He probably sees me as the lone cold spot in a room full of flames.
I feel like a *Soul Train* dancer among the crippled and lame,
Though I am just enjoying a soft drink
While watching the games.

There is football on the flat screens.
I see ladies with nice bodies but their souls appear mean,
Turned off by the men and women trying to get in their jeans.
Folk being walked by their liquor while making scenes,
Eyes plotting schemes.
The atmosphere is forming wet realities and dreams
From the songs played through the karaoke machine.
Songbirds with broken beaks are trying to sing,
Led on by libation and loud screams.
Two tables are about to fight over their teams.
I'm offered a shot because my mind seems too keen.
I almost accept, but I don't want to lose my sheen.
Women glance, but there's no interest in my gleam.
It probably reminds them of police beams.
I don't mind because all I can offer is some C.R.E.A.M:

Christ Rules Everything around Me.
Yes, that's what it means.
I can't judge because I was once part of what I've seen.
My freedom and I just want to shine in a darkly lit room
While enjoying some wings.

The guy returns as the games conclude.
He says, "Dude, you still okay?"
I reply, "Standing in faith, setting the bar.
Let me call you a taxi. You won't make it far, my friend."
He answers, "You're probably right."
I help him dodge physical death again,
So his soul and spirit still have a chance.
The devil didn't have all the fun that night.

LADY LUST

She's on a prowl,
Roaming, unaware of herself
But aware of what she wants,
Layers of fronts
That should be peeled
But oftentimes are not.
We skip the cold and warm,
Zoned in on the hot spots:
The sexy walk is approaching us.
The sexy talk is promoting us,
A few drinks … a toast to us.
Already?
What's the rush?

Shhh… Hush.
Don't you like my eyes?
My skin tone?
My thighs?

I mean, yes, but …
I like my prize
At the bottom of the box,
A pleasant surprise.

Stop being a wuss.
Be like other guys.
In this regard,
Love on a platter.
I want yours.
You know you want my heart.

You sure you want to start at the end?
Finished before we begin?
I'm not a track star.
You want a sport or a man?

I want both.
Bite my hook
And jump in my boat.

Think I'll pass, Lady Lust.
I'm going to swim deeper.
I'm looking for a mermaid
To share my coast.

WORLD OF FREEDOM

I tried building a world of my own,
But after I built it,
I was still overcrowded, alone.
That's because I tried using
What was already full blown
In my mind.
In essence, I wasn't building at all,
Just relocating my thoughts,
Like a trailer home
With a leaky roof.
My blueprints and proofs
Were as reliable as pudding
Between bricks.
That meant I was still a product
Of the world around me,
A part of the plague,
Membership with the sick,
A zombie with a handsome mask.
My pants didn't hang off my ass,
But I was a follower of my d**k
With no clue on how to build my
Own world within,
One that would stick
Like Gorilla Glue and wisdom
Injected into my brain with a syringe

Until I was left with no choice
But to destroy, then rebuild
Every piece of fragmented foundation.
Its fragile frame was frantically killed.
Frivolous friends … dead!
Freakish acts … dead!
Fraudulent support … dead!
As God is my contractor,
I never felt more alive, alone.
Now I roam as though I got a home
To retract to when the dome
Of this world collapses.
Perhaps it's because
I've built my very own
World of freedom.

LONELY EMOTIONS

Excuse me if I appear not to need anything or anybody.
It's just that loneliness misled me once.
I constantly followed it into liquor stores,
Rotations of blunts,
And subsequently down a dark alley.
All I could see of myself was a name: Rod Hunt.

Excuse me if my emotions appear emotionless.
It's just that I carried others'
Bags for so long that now I don't even want
My own tugging at my face or sleeves.
Plus I'm naturally my mom's child.
Outside the scolding looks of discipline,
She gave me only straight faces and smiles
With occasional tears.

I now walk ahead of loneliness, which helps
Keep my emotions tamed.
It's not that I don't need anything or body.
I just don't need them for me to be sane.
That means I can stand being misunderstood,
But if you want to get to know me,
I really wish you would.
Please, ignore my look of indifference.
I'll let you meet my lonely emotions
Just like neighbors should.

CALL ... WAITING

"My friends don't deserve my friendship,"
I've often said to myself.
I'm conquering loneliness by the minute,
And my thoughts are
Showing up in my
Actions like a cure
Through an epidemic,
But I choose to defend your position:
One that is noble
But robs us
Of reciprocity,
My closest friend, who's simply hard to befriend.
That small spot of intermittent loneliness I protect.
A mixture of selfishness and concern
Sets in when I know
Something unknown
Has you down,
Not up enough to confirm any thoughts
Of me, as I go from
A back burner to a
Place not even on
The stove, unable
To provide warmth.

I have to wait in the lobby of frustration
Until further notice …? … ???!!! … ???
But unless you send word that I should go
And never retract, I'll
Stay put, relax, read
Myself until you call
Me back …
Or from this point, first.

FIRE OF TRUST

I trust in God fully;
Therefore, all people are trustworthy
Even when they're not.
I trust them to be who they'll be.
God will reveal what I need to see
And help me spot the snake grass
Among my garden of fruitful friends,
To be picked with love and forgiveness
And stacked in a pile of enemies
But burned with a fire of life nonetheless,
Free to rise with the smoke that they blow.
I had high hopes when they came.
I'm ecstatic to see them go.
God bless.

CONQUEROR

I want to be the god God promised me I could be.

I want to stand above the abnormalities of the norm.

I want to walk in a room of strangers and get strange looks,

    Not because of my looks, but because of the radiation of

    God's Spirit through mine.

I want to walk in the orderliness that my clothing and home suggest.

I want my blessings and I to represent each other well.

I want to lead my natural feelings and emotions like a major leads his troops,

Getting supernatural victories.

I want to keep my thoughts, words, and actions controlled and humbled

Before and after my victories.

I want my actions to do the talking while I'm walking.

I want to lead people away from their default selves, …

    To whom they are designed to be.

I want to wear the full armor of faith so tightly that it appears I can hardly breathe,

    But in essence, I'm capturing life.

I want to be able to walk through Satan's battlefield and be the last man standing,

    Calmly holding his sword at his neck

    With my armor still in check.

I want to be a conqueror from another world conquering the world around me—

More than a conqueror, actually …

The one St. Paul said I could be.

PART 3

FAITH: BACK AHEAD
OF MY TIME

But by faith we eagerly await through the Spirit
the righteousness for which we hope.

—Galatians 5:5

SOUL CONFIRMATION

In church as a kid
To me, some of the praise just didn't seem real.
However, Mama is the truest woman I know.
She and the mothers of the church made me wonder
What it was they could feel:
Shakes of comfort as genuine as leather massage chairs,
Tears as real as rotating showerheads of love.
As Mama's hand held mine at altar call,
Talking tongues were remotely shared,
Whispers of foreign English.
I heard it, but I couldn't reach it.
I sought it, but I couldn't seek it.
Maybe I wasn't guilty enough to speak it.
Whatever it was, she was trying to teach it.
Knew my birth pass to heaven wouldn't remain sufficient.
She knew her hands couldn't always serve as my ticket.
She didn't ever want me to be a stranger to God's will.
Recently, we held hands and prayed before my surgery.
I released those same tears and chills.
My soul says the Spirit of Christ is real.
People overlook what they can't or don't want to understand.
I'm thankful Mama held my head straight on Sundays and revivals.
My clip-on ties set up the arrival of the ties I have as a man.

MIRROR OF BELIEFS

Hey, I know that dude in the mirror.

I know where he's going when he leaves,

What he wants to achieve,

What he believes,

What he stands for.

He can't stand to deceive.

He thrives for what's right.

He wants to be real like the breaths he breathes,

Infatuated with patience like a cool breeze.

Looks at love as the fix for any disease.

Believes death only appears to succeed.

Believes Life reappears to intercede,

Imperfect like a late-blooming seed.

Prays to perform perfect deeds.

Prays not to worry about wants and needs.

Prays things be revealed like a Facebook news feed.

Realizes he didn't make himself

But realizes he can break himself.

He wants to return to the mirror as a better man … indeed.

HEAVEN ON EARTH

I hung out in death's living room
So honestly; it wasn't because I was afraid of hell.
I just got tired of the hell on earth.
Now that I fear God, I'm closer to a human being,
On earth as it is in heaven.
And hell is still no more of a concern to me
Than a spanking is to an innocent child,
Though I'm concerned about my siblings in God.

Many are like I was and who I'm trying not to be …
Trying the perfect mixture of good deeds and dirty habits,
But positives don't make up for negatives.
They only highlight their power of reducing souls, …
Trying to maintain a feeling of honesty and realness,
But not all honesty and reality are the truth.

Willing to flip a coin on the afterlife,
Thinking they control the toss like their lives,
Half believers think their halves control God's—
That is, until they're in need.
Then it's "Jesus, take the wheel."

Many are afraid of death but not hell.
Why fear if the worst is back to dust …
Or if we believe we're heaven bound regardless?
Family and friends will be fine after we're gone.
God will intervene from His half and secure them, right?

Heaven and hell are in a troubled marriage on earth.
Hell is the tolerated man of the house.
The fear of hell in trying to save souls is dead.
Pride is powerful enough to accept hell on earth,
Even more powerful to take its chances elsewhere.
It needs to see and experience the great divorce,
Heaven at its highest earthly elevation,
Where souls defeat death and fly above cardinals.
Heaven felt down here keeps our eyes up there,
In a place where we really don't have to fear hell,
And we don't have to wait until it's too late.

STRUGGLE OF BEAUTY

I don't want to get so caught up in the cause
That I forget about the effects of true living.

I don't want to put beauty on pause
Due to the ugliness this world is giving.

If the wind tries to push me back,
I'll let God's reign soak my soul.

If my daily plans come under attack,
I'll patiently await God's assigned goals.

If my home theater won't pick up the game,
I'll watch the squirrels jump from limb to limb.

Life and leisure are simple yet far from plain
When complexities are handed over to Elohim.

When I'm shot in the head with hate,
I'll return fire to the heart with kindness.

Most things aren't even worth a debate.
Faith sees goodness in blindness.

Life can be a struggle,
Though not so much when the struggle is not.

There's even beauty in a juggle
When balance is situated in the right spot.

Envision sunshine walking with a clear cover of flesh,
So bright that the darkness can't smother.

Picture the sunshine rising upon death,
Coming back later to reshape that dusty cover.

That's beauty worth struggling for.

HIS LIGHT

His goodness is good.
His freedom is free.
I can have it all
For the price of all of me.

His will be done,
I willingly pray.
I feel defeated
When my will gets its way.

I'm starstruck by the moon.
I'm in awe of God's Son.
I see Him in everything.
I feel Him within and among.

I long for His power.
I suffer for His peace.
I thirst for His wisdom,
A hunger I care not to cease.

My walk is by faith,
Not always a stroll in the park.
But even the jungle's path is lit;
His light is never dark.

MEDIOCRE MINISTRY

I grew up in it.
I always knew where the church was,
Around the corner from the liquor store.
They both led me to my soul and spirit,
Yet had I not grown up in the church,
My soul would still be saturated in gin.

Like many,
It would've been hard to contend
    with what I had within,
Viewed as having more lost causes
    than wins,
A place where enemies can pretend
    to be friends for a day.
The rest of the week they can lend
    their ears to others
    about each other,
But with no regards to what the Lord has to say.
Liars with honest faces on display,
Holy folk can be filled with holes in their faith.
Functionless functions to those outside,
Running those in, out.

Doubt of man gives folks doubts about God.

I had to break this chain to realize I was chained.

I overlooked man to see that God wasn't a facade.

Real men of God helped me across the quicksand
    of myself and mediocrity.

God speaks through men.

I don't want His voice tainted, coming from me.

I pray that my actions don't succumb to
    mediocre ministry.

I don't mind going back to the liquor store
    but not for liquor.

I would look to uncap my soul … and pour.

FAITH OF AN OAK TREE

Staring out the blinds as I recline,
My mind isn't exactly clear,
But neither is the sunshine.
We're being patient with a dark cloud,
The rare chilliness of the spring.
The mood of the day wants to join mine.
I wish I could join the birds as they sing,
But they seem content with silence as well.
The green leaves on the oak tree
Are the joy that sustains me.
The slight breeze they play in
Is the hope that I want to stay in
As we grow farther apart from this world.
I realize things have to be left behind;
To rise, some things just can't be compromised.
May my faith be still like the oak tree.
I give myself totally to Thee.

LOST MIRACLES

We're miracles walking through miracles,
Designed reasons walking through seasons,
Born with a default chip on our shoulders,
One that many are never able to get over.

Buried as free moral soldiers of their own appetites,
Unpleasurable fights over pleasure:
Empty treasure chests searching for diamonds,
Bodies are looking for elevation in the *mine*fields.
Their spirits bottomed up and faced down,
Begging Satan to kiss them where the sun can't shine.
Even the moon isn't much more than a mystery over a glass of wine.
Stars, nothing but celebrities that they fantasize and envy under,
Outrunning hope,
Following wonder,
May not trip over everything but will fall for anything,
Unable to find peace with lightning and thunder.
Animals bark over what they can't stop,
Ignoring what they can,
Finding it easier to be apes with common sense
Than wise men who understand.

They can be supernaturally one with nature,
Joyous miracles walking through miracles,
Designed reasons walking through seasons.
I dare them to bend their knees and give themselves to Jesus.

WITHIN HIS REALM

I know when I'm in.
I can feel when I'm out,
Out of a cloud of confidence,
Into the gravitational pull of doubt.

The pull of the Lord's hand prevents my drop after my fall.
What a strain having to regain my position of faith.
I know turbulence comes with elevation.
It's much less minus the unnecessary disturbance of pace.

Faith used to feel like what a box does to a homeless man.
I felt freer sleeping under the bridge to my home.
I eventually learned how to be still.
I rose from boxed up, across the bridge, to a soul that's fully grown.

My comfort is sometimes discomfort in waiting.
Death's living room looks so enticing at times.
The patience of the heart can be invaded.
Temporal desires are cancers of the mind.

Hold on! Hold on to God's unchanging hand.
I'm far from trying to snatch away from Him.
I don't want to take His strength for granted.
I'm so high now that it's easier just to stay … within His realm.

OFF THE CHAINLESS PLANK

Why are you mad at my chosen path?

You seem to want to blame me

For the insecurities of your own.

Would you feel better to know that I suffered and still suffer to walk this path?

I walk with ease because I've handed God my hardships.

What type of freedom are you trying to make me see?

Is it the freedom to be meaningless so I can be useful mostly to myself?

If I were to pass right now, what would I miss that I haven't already experienced?

More sex partners or positions … I'll pass.

Higher forms of artificial highs … I'll pass.

A larger friends' list … I'll pass.

Another black president … I'll pass.

More democracy … I'll pass.

A better dance or political party … I'll pass.

Are these types of things freedom?

If not, what is? What are you freeing me from, and where are we going?

Historical debates became useless once

Christ started using my present as eternity.

I don't have time to harbor hate over what I've been delivered from.

Oh, so I'm brainwashed?

Can you be my ultimate sacrifice and wash me with your blood

Until one of history's bombs destroys my earthly home?

Then show me what all the biblical symbolism is about in the afterlife?

Oh, so I'm blind as well?

No, I choose to believe in the unseen.

Excuse me for being dumb enough

To think I was made for more than this world,

For thinking I'm a spirit with a flesh and not the reverse.

I'm really not interested in being the most

Intelligent, reasonable, or fiscally rich …

On this new-world slave ship,

Where all races are riding illusions of comfort and discomfort.

Can you give me spiritual blessings and riches?

Smother my useless wisdom and complaints?

When the ship sinks, I want my spirit to rise off my chainless plank.

Can you lift me up like Christ already has?

I didn't think so. Have a pleasant day.

ETERNAL WITNESS

As a child, my foundation was built;
Mama chose Christ as our family's contractor.
As I grew blessed from innocence to the less tender age of guilt
And a lackluster behavior toward my appointed Savior,
My services were weighed down by skepticism of His worthiness.

I was a freshman in college with fresh ideas of finding my own way;
But God saw my heart beforehand, my unwillingness to stay
Still behind His will instead of my own.
I picked curiosity up on my way out of my home state of mind.
I didn't forget the Bible the church gave me as a gift;
I intentionally left it behind.
Explore the world on one straight and narrow path?
That thought made me laugh as if life were a joke.
I developed perceptions through the evil one who often spoke,
Indirectly through my peers or direct whispers in my ears.
I was told that G.O.D. meant "Gaining One's Definition."
It was stupid to look for a live God in a dead book like the Bible.
Supposedly, God was mere intelligence and faith, what you made
of it.
I searched the library for worldly relevance to add to my idols.
I learned to live and let live, unknowingly dying and letting die.
Individually, experience alone was supposed to guide us all.
We were the gatekeepers of our sins.
We controlled our own uprisings and our own downfalls.
Down I felt as theories led to no peace.
I then searched for my cool in a pool of booze,

Swimming with a cloud of weed smoke hovering above;
I mistook lust for real love, the unnecessary push and shove
For an escape.
I was a liberal arts major, too minor spiritually,
And too tolerant in flesh and mind to even graduate;

I was a grown man headed back home,
Too broke and feeling too alone to make it on my own.
I was too far gone mentally to consider spiritual atonement;
Time and money was still spent getting bent, sadly content
With darkness; my childhood blinds stayed closed to sunshine
Like a vampire with artificial happiness during the night.
Thank God my people were the praying kind.
As I was too old for the belt, word was sent to God to whip my behind
To where I needed to be, because I was clueless;
While walking around on this life support,
I was a poster boy for falling short of glory of any sort.
Yet blessings still came with disguises and distortion in my eyes;
My soul was lost. My flesh was my guide.

Pushing thirty, my constant dead ends drove me to my knees
As I envisioned that old path I was raised to believe.
No longer just about me, my seed proceeded to sprout.
I had to get up, get out, and do something about the doubt
Overwhelming me; thought processes changed,
Started making gains according to the world's standards.
Had my own place, my own cash, but still I thought I had my own
Brain as I thanked God while also saying no thanks.
I acknowledged His presence but still wanted to coach my own game:
Him, His Son, the Holy Spirit, and whoever could be my assistants.
Brushing the surface of belief yet still lame with ignorance,
I tried to wipe my impurities off for keepsakes,
To use like fine china on special evenings, my stream weaving
In and out of consciousness as moderation proved its death.
Too many exhaled breaths were still accompanied by smoke,
Too many sips of gin to smother the occasional chokes;
I was blinded and stranded by lies and false hopes
Of getting out of this neck of the woods, into the heart of real life:

I longed for who is and what purpose the image in the mirror serves;
I wanted that joy that shines during simple times,
Like enjoying company without the help of vodka or wine;
I wanted the joy that faces loneliness with the same genuine smile.
I longed for the joy that sustains under pointed fingers of disdain
and doubt.
I wanted to discontinue the masks I wore to survive in this world.

Distant from this wish, I wore disguises to hide my disgust of feeling
Like a homeless roamer with a fancy buggy and a few bucks in my
sock.
I made an occasional pulpit stop on Easter or Mother's Day to drop
Some spare change while full change was improbable like a flame
With no oxygen;
I was a dead man walking with chains and a few last words in his
mouth.
Those words now come in the form of a prayer asking for the way,
Because my ways seem awfully wayward;
The answer I get is the one I've been receiving since the beginning.
I'm praying for resistance toward multiple choices.
Lord, give me strength to block out voices that want
To mix righteousness with sinning for the benefit of the latter.
My hope has been based on the color green and other things seen.
My life has been like my money.
The more I've tried to save my own,
The more I've lost like unrecalled dreams.

Tired of trying to fill emptiness with bitter doctrines of sweetness,
I now rely on the sweet words of Christ for completeness.
He's the supplier of the joy that lives through bitter times.
My mind is no longer looking to challenge God's words;
I'm searching for refinement line after line.
With my heart in His word and Him in me, my past is my past,
And my present is eternity, … eternal witness.

PART 4

DISCOVERY OF REAL LOVE

Three things will last forever—faith, hope, and
love—and the greatest of these is love.

—1 Corinthians 13:13

TRULY ONE LOVE

I can't stop thinking about the love of God, and I don't want to.
Never had a love that continued to stand even
     when I felt unloved.
Had loves I ran to that ran to me for those quick stances,
But when the rush was hushed, they were broken like
unsuccessful picket lines, back to square one and done.

Never had a love that sustained me through worry,
     a dark room, and a thunderstorm at night … all at once.
Imagine being in love with a storm so much that you
     hear it telling you that everything is fine.
Never had a love that brought my imagination to a
     life of supernatural proportions.

Never had a love that truly made me feel guilty
     about all my other loves.
Most of them got along, … even the conflicting ones.
As long as the interests weren't exposed, I could
     carry on uninterrupted.
I'm thankful my soul has been interrupted.

Never had a love that enhanced my good times
    without ever having regrets the next morning,
Without me having to wake to feel the invisible
    chains around my ankles: the ones I was numb
    to as I danced with Ms. Tanqueray the night prior,
The rattles that blended in so well with the music
    of Sodom.

My love-making disasters were natural occurrences:
What exactly is "making love"?
Love has already been made.
There was love before light.
The light has to be used to find it.
Love can be found in the darkness.
It can't be found with darkness.
God is love.
Christ is the Son and the light.
He wants us to hand Him our natural loves.
He wants to filter them and make them conquerors:
True love for self,
True love for others,
Better relations,
Heavenly worlds.
I found it, and I believe …
It's truly one love …
That makes all others succeed.

HOOD CITY LOVE

I wanted your athletic ability and to hold my pencil like you did, …
Your slanted handwriting, your popularity, your humor.
I wanted a big brother like yours. I wanted to go with you
To Atlanta to see your big brother play in the Waycross High
basketball state championship game in '85. I once tried to
Shoot my jumper like you, walk like you. Your laugh was different.
I once tried it, but I sounded stupid. I wanted your smile, but I didn't
Have that perfect flaw on my top lip like you did. We teased
You about it, but deep down I wanted it. I wanted a chest like yours.
You had already started working out. I wanted a weight bench
In my backyard, too. I wanted your height. You were only a month
Older than I, but I looked up to you.

I guess that's why I didn't trade you my new Fat Boy shoestrings
For your "rappin" soundtrack cassette. I felt you already had it all.
I wish I would've just given you the strings, because you gave me
Something far more valuable … friendship, brotherhood.
You used to get onto me for not taking my street ball intensity to
The real court. I would be scared to face you at school when I only
Scored two points on my rec team the weekend prior. You would shake
Your head as if to say, "You know you better than that."
I remember how excited I felt when I found out your sixth-grade football

team won the midget championship and you put up the only score. My football days were over by then. I wanted your heart and passion. I remember feeling bad one time after an older kid tried to pick a fight With you, and I just stood there, scared. You were a good kid, so you didn't bite.

I would have given anything for that fire you had in your eyes, though. That kid was just jealous. He wanted what you had too.

No day goes by without a thought of you.

To reflect on my life is to reflect on yours.

You never stopped living within me.

I remember I saw you in a dream once, and you said, "What's up, Rod?"

I replied, "Chillin'." You told me, "No man. You need to be living."

You were right, and I thank God that I am now.

You even got something now that I want someday, and that's heaven.

I'm determined to see you again. Happy birthday, Eric, and Hood City loves you.

By the way, tell Lynnwood we said "what's good."

FRIENDS FINALLY

Forgive me, homeboy, for using you the way I did.
I brought my demons to your crib,
Many times unannounced,
And didn't bounce
Until I was like a kid who had to be called home by his mama.
Way past the streetlights,
I filled your living room and nights
Up with death.
We called it chilling … the gin, juice, and weed smoke
That accompanied our breaths
As we spoke between tokes and chokes
About how good we felt at that moment.
But life was a bitch.
I know you and yours always enjoyed my company.
I promptly
Accepted your invites to return,
But my soul yearns
For forgiveness for what I took from you
Or rather what I gave. "What's that?" you ask.
I gave you reasoning, ambition I didn't even have, luck.
I gave you thumbs-up on that chick you wanted to cut.
I suggested material things for bling.
"What's wrong with all of that?" you ask.
I never spoke of faith … So everything!

My homey, I definitely want to apologize
For using you after this realization.
I secretly sought salvation
While openly displaying life as some big vacation
We had to find time to work on.
I know how hard you saw me work,
But it's not my job I speak of. Listen!
For once, pay attention
To something other than the mention
Of money, clothes, and hoes.
For me that stuff is frozen in suspension.
I began regretting your admission,
But most of all my willingness to enter.
When I needed a validation for my sin,
I came to you, my main man,
My favorite sinner.
And that's the cup in which my apology lies.
If you've noticed a difference,
You now know the cause of my gradual distance.
It's necessary but doesn't have to mean the end.
Where do we go from here?
Since my faith is a relationship, not just a religion,
I'm cool with being homeys,
But let's start fresh by really being friends.
No, unfold your fist. Let's shake hands.
I love you, man.

LOVE SHE NEVER HAD

She will think of my love on her deathbed,

The type of love she never lived,

The type of love that never changes,

The type of love she didn't think existed.

She went through so many artificial forms that when she met the true spirit

    of love, she thought my screws were untwisted.

She wants true love but can't see it through the sex.

Even when it's the last thing on her mind, she can't fathom how love can

    be first and then sex next.

That's because I was talking about the love of God between two people,

Not the Steve Harvey ninety-day rule.

We could've waited 180 days and still come out looking like fools

    in the long run,

And what I feel is rare but has never been new under the sun.

In fact, God designed it before mankind started f**king for fun.

And there's wonder as to why relationships and marriages

    are being tossed by the tons.

It's because the love of God is not at the forefront.

They're done before they even get started,

Unequally yoked or not at all, disorderly stroked.

Perceptions are commonly wisdom retarded.

She told me what I'm looking for in a woman is too strict.
But first of all, I'm not looking for anybody.
Second, what I want and need God will provide.
Therefore, what I want and need right now I've already got.
I don't have to place standards on women.
I place them on myself.
That alone leaves women intrigued on the spot,
Yet it's something many are powerless to match or do anything about,
A pull that has nothing to do with me but the Spirit inside.
She wanted me inside her but didn't realize she had so far to go.
Even if she had success in her immediate quest,
    it would've exploded in our faces.

This world has people placing what feels right in all the wrong places.
The devil will take the sweetest and prettiest faces
and turn them into hoes in the classiest clothes.
Got them roaming around, unknowingly looking to break up families,
Keeping men and women enslaved, cracking celibacy codes.

To counter this, my aim is to be a godly man with godly stances.

If and when God sees fit, He'll give me a godly woman to enhance
    my romances of real life.

We'll sport our armor of faith together against deceit.

Our souls and spirits will make love a million times before our bodies
even meet.

Regardless of how long I've known her, when she arrives, we'll greet.

We'll fellowship perhaps over a bite to eat.

I'll tell her that Christ heads my life.

She'll smile as if the first connection is complete.

Her smile will make me smile.

We'll share the innocence and freedom of child's play for a while.

Neither of us has to rush, because we're on God's time.

The world is just a footstool where we place our feet.

We'll expose secrets and problems

And worship and pray together

Until we're ready for the battle of commitment.

We receive God's grace to stay together: holy matrimony.

We know for sure that sex is more than physical.

It's anchored in God's spiritual love.

Heaven opens wider, and we decide to lie together,

Sex exactly how it was created to be.

In His realm, there's no such thing as sexual incompatibility.

But the lost beauty will think of my love on her deathbed:

A love she never lived,

A love that never changes,

A love she didn't think existed,

A love she never had, but somehow … she now misses it.

GUTTERS OF PARADISE

It's a damn shame how beauty can be overlooked and underappreciated,
How diamonds can be neglected,
All to brag about how we made it to home plate.
What's wrong with spending a little time on first base,
Even if the first spark is like a hit out of the park?
What's wrong with basking in that woman's voice over the phone,
Which seems to get softer way past dark?

We share stories of substance, joke about the clowns who couldn't
keep her heart.
She tells me that she's painting her toes,
And that brings back memories of her pedicure
Peeping out the stilettos she wore the night we met.
Yet I don't want to spoil paradise by thinking of its gutters.
My vision is on x-ray as I zoom in on her ethos.
I'm interested in the spirit of her voice, not thoughts of lustful stutters.

Sex is a natural thing, but so is garbage juice flowing down gutters,
And bodies and souls spread too thin and fast
Only end up in the trash.
Players are on the prowl with fancy, Oscar the Grouch costumes and
masks.
Dames down for games are trading shots in the ass for shots in a
glass,
Everybody playing each other and himself or herself,
Being animals we were made to be rulers over.

I tried to be a faithful animal once, but I turned on my masters.

Now I'm a faithful and free man, walking the beaches of paradise,

Enjoying all sights and sounds, hourglasses and laughter.

I don't have to look for sand, and I didn't bring any with me.

I'm enjoying my newfound freedom and manhood,

A mental land where true love is at the forefront,

A place where I don't have to be drunk

To say every woman is beautiful.

Even when the world argues that some don't look good,

It's a place where I can truly say I love women,

Without it having anything to do with her garden or my piece of wood,

A place where I can be real about where I stand,

And she can stand by me, or I can just be misunderstood.

Let her go elsewhere if she just has to have her apple bitten at the tick of her tock.

I made it past the temptations of Eden.

I'm now in paradise, relaxing on God's watch,

And I wasn't freed just to be led to another trap.

Gentlemen, it's not freedom to have fountains all over town to tap.

You're only sporting balls and chains for ankle bracelets.

Face it …

You're walking along the gutters of paradise

Along with garbage trucks, hood rats, and mice.

And according to a favorite quote of mine,

"An ignorant child who wants to go on

Making mud pies in a slum because he

Cannot imagine what is meant

By an offer of a holiday at the sea,

We are far too easily pleased."[1]

As for me, I like to see women on their knees as well,

But sucking up, begging, and pleading with God to release them from their hell.

Maybe one day God will bless me with the essence of her freedom's presence,

And we'll eventually get nasty on the seashore instead of in the gutters.

Until then, my freedom and I will enjoy these waves of pleasure,

Even during a flood.

My faith welcomes all types of weather.

---

[1] C.S. Lewis, *The Weight of Glory and Other Addresses*, (Sydney: HarperCollins, 1949), 26.

ARE YOU READY?

Are you ready for a man who doesn't treat
All his feelings the same way,
Embracing some while locking the others
Away like bastardly misfits,
Although none of them ever truly get their
Way ... unless it's God approved?

Are you ready for a man who likes fine things
But desperately looks to rely on finer things,
Eternal, that won't rust or turn to dust?
A man who peeps only at his watch for
Earthly deadlines while he gets closer
To forever?

Are you ready for a man whose idea of a
Free spirit is one that is free from
The pull of the flesh, realizing that the
Free merging of the two can be like
Too much wind on an innocent and
Harmless flame, causing it to go out
Or grow harmfully out of control?

Are you ready for a man who thinks deeply
And beyond, not just to sound different
But because he sees and feels something
Out there that he's deeply attracted to—and
He's attracted only to things on the surface
That resemble that vision?

Are you ready for a humbly imperfect man
Who looks to stay on the airway to
Perfection, ... perfect in the sense of having
All imperfections accounted for
Improvements? One who's escaped the idea
Of inviting his past ghosts in for toasts
Because he now controls them and
Not them him? One who wants his actions
To match his heart so he doesn't deceive
Those who are close?

Are you ready for that endangered good
Man who thrives to be really good through
The voice of his Maker, realizing that God
Doesn't speak to his logic but to his faith?
And he aims to follow by any means?
Worldly woman, are you really ready
For the aggravation?

GOLD COIN TOSS

I pray for you like I pray for myself—
For spiritual strength and wealth,
All that we're promised to gain,
No strings dangling on my requests.
I realize the zone I chose with you.
I'm secure in where my heart rests.
God is the official over my doubts,
Hope on each side of a gold coin's chest.

Tails for continued friendship,
Heads for a higher level.
My first prayer was the first toss.
Those thereafter control the spin in the wind
So that hope is not totally lost.
And while the coin spins,
My river of reciprocation flows,
Making sure not to flood zones that need to grow,
Secrets free for only you and God to know.

I look up and see tails controlling the land.
That's cool. God has the toss fixed. Either way,
There'll be vast amounts of spiritual wealth in the end.
Then, if I can,
I'll toss the gold coin again.
I'll always be a true friend, a friend of truth …
No ordinary man.

FEEL-GOOD FAMILY

Don't it feel good

To get together with no black suits, dresses, and hats involved?

To share these couple of days together with no problems to solve?

To be able to drop all titles,

Except those we take pride in holding until the earth seizes to revolve

And beyond,

Like mother, daughter, father, son … niece, nephew,

Or just that friend of the family, to name a few?

Don't it feel good

To know that we didn't have to consult with a preacher to do this?

All it took was God's grace for us to gather and reminisce

On past times, the renewal of old stories.

I don't know about you, but they never seem to bore me.

I never met them,

But it seems to me Aunt Hattie and Mattie were women destined for glory.

It feels good to see that glory manifested here today.

Everyone is living comfortably during these current struggles

In his or her own unique way.

This reminds me of the reunion in Columbus back in the eighties.

I was just a bashful kid back in those days.

Don't it feel good

To see me as a man now with something to say?

Don't it feel good

To see any relative you haven't seen in a while?

You can't quite remember his or her name,
But you know that's so-and-so's child.
"Boy, you done put on some weight!"
"Yeah, I'm working on that, but today put some ribs on my plate!"

Don't it feel good
To let bygones be bygones while we catch up on days gone by,
To let loose and be you without questions of what and why?
Let all acts be accompanied by elation.
If not, let's give God our aggravations.
We never know what any of us will be facing
When the next vacation rolls around.

Let's enjoy these sights and sounds of nature that surround us
And let all fuss be harmonious.
So when those who didn't make it ask,
We can give a positive testimonial.
Today let's renew that colonial bond,
Those times before our investment funds ranked higher than
family fun,
And do just that, family. Have loving fun and fun loving,
And feel good doing it.

JOE PETE

Uncle Joe,

You know I could've called you Uncle Bubba.

That's what I used to hear Mu and Big Mama call you.

No matter how tall you got,

They never planned to let you outgrow the country.

You never knew of the talks Big Mama and I had,

But she was glad of what you had become.

There weren't too many black men earning degrees where you came from.

At the age when her mind wondered,

She envisioned her family all sitting together in a government-built home.

She spoke of it as reality, not some dream she had.

Even as a child, it seemed so far fetched and kind of sad,

Though the older I get, the more sense it makes.

The government was God, and home is through those heavenly gates.

Now nothing is sad about that.

I can see Big Mama smiling now.

Uncle Joe,

I could've even called you Uncle Clarence,

A good son of a good man, by which you were named.

This name was casually placed in my mind at a young age.

Yet it sounded too formal for your obvious ways.

I'm sure that's what the professionals called you at the office.

Your old classmates asked about Clarence when they found out I was your sister's son.

Those were just curious outsiders trying to peep in through the window.

They never knew Clarence like I knew Uncle Joe Pete.

That name puts me in the back of a Cadillac, watching you brush your hair,

Taking me and my cousins to a rap concert at the Jacksonville Coliseum.

Heavy D was your favorite of the acts. Remember that?

It takes me back to that brown bag of forty-five records you gave me

And that brown Kangol hat you bought me from Ice Man,

Because I liked to plunder through your collection over the summer.

You used to come to the family cookouts like the evening breeze,

Those being some of the few times my basketball and I took a break from the heat.

A Chek soda and the dap you gave made the day complete.

My appreciation runs deeper than my memories,
And I speak of the past not because it's too late.
Your history has never been my forever more than now.
Along with my father, you were one of the ones who showed me how
To stick to my roots and Hunt for the Hills,
Even when circumstances surround me with sour deals.
Family, I know this all feels so surreal, but keep that dream alive
Because his struggle is complete.
I know I'll never let him die.
We love you, Uncle Joe Pete.

LIVING LIKE SHE LOVED

In my dream
You were begging and pleading for me to do something.
I awoke, unsure of what exactly.
Reflecting on your life, I can probably guess
You want me to give my all to God.
I remember when I had many gods.
You told me they would get old and perish.
You were basically telling me to cherish the everlasting.

You probably want me to love my family unconditionally.
You told me once that it didn't matter whether I never checked on you.
You would always check on me.
You didn't want me to forget that you loved me after you were gone.
That was about fifteen years before God called you home.
I'll never forget
That you loved me or the last time we spoke.
You, Kaylee Mae, and I held hands and spoke with God.
That was your idea.
I told you I would keep you in my prayers later on.
In so many words, you asked, "Why put off until tomorrow
What is desperately calling to be taken care of today?"

Today
I'll give my all to God.
I'll love my family like the blood of Christ,
Unconditionally … like you and your life taught me.
Aunt Betty, rest in peace. Enjoy your new life in heaven.
We love you.

BEST FOR LAST (TRIBUTE TO MY GRANDMA, MU)

It was a Sunday morning, like any other,

I sat in my pickup and mumbled a thankful prayer for strength

Before pulling off to entertain duty's call. Woke up feeling small,

But the higher the sun rose, the more I was filled with feelings of having it all.

"I'm glad my worst days are behind me," my Facebook status read,

But by early afternoon, a call shifted my tune,

Saying that my grandma had started her final rest.

She'd lived a long life, but that didn't stop the knife of disappointment

From entering the left side of my chest, the deflation of my day.

But during the forty-minute drive home,

An inflation of memories was enough to confirm that everything was okay.

Nothing's bad about the joy I felt as a child

Whenever I spotted that city bus stop on Moncrief,

The landmark that told me Mu was right around the corner and up the street,

Most likely rocking in her seat on the porch. As we pulled up,

Her smile would be as long as the concrete slab that led to her steps.

Speaking of which, I learned at an early age that I'd better watch mine.

Like her good cooking, she was a mixture of sugar but mostly spice.

She wasn't concerned about killing you nicely if you crossed her threadlike line.

She was the first to tell me my face was getting fat

But the first to remind me that I was still a fine-looking young man.

My attention to outward details isn't hard to understand

If you've ever witnessed her fine Sunday hats and dresses,

The gleam on her neck and hands, which are probably manicured as
we speak.

She also kept the sparkle renewed on her soul.

Mu could be highly opinionated at times,

But for the final say-so, she knew where to go:

Straight to the blood that gave death its final breath,

So that Mu's last wouldn't be the end,

So that the memories within me wouldn't be in vain

But stand as paintings of eternity.

This may be a time for a few tears,

But they don't have to be joyless and filled with uncertainty.

I've grown to believe that with faith in God,

I can wake up every morning, feeling my worst days are in the past.

Family and friends, Mu is bringing her paintings to life.

God always saves the best for last.

Printed in the United States
By Bookmasters